BLACK MAN WHITE HOUSE

THE STRUGGLE IS REAL

ERIC REESE

Copyright © 2019 by Eric Reese

All rights reserved.

No part of this book may be reproduced in any form or by any electronic or mechanical means, including information storage and retrieval systems, without written permission from the author, except for the use of brief quotations in a book review.

CONTENTS

Black Power	1
Slavery	5
The Underground Railroad	9
The Dred Scott Decision	13
The Harlem Renaissance	17
Booker T. Washington	21
George Washington Carver	25
Harriet Tubman	29
The Triumph At The Berlin Olympics	33
Jackie Robinson	37
A Troubled Time	41
Affirmative Action	45
Brown Versus The Board Of Education	49
Rosa Parks	53
Martin Luther King, Jr.	57
Martin Luther King Jr.'s Dream	61
Thurgood Marshall	65
The Halls Of Power	69
The Proud Black American Soldier	72
Laughter That Heals	76
The Thirteenth Amendment	80
The Fifteenth Amendment	84
The Rainbow Coalition	88
Afterword	93

BLACK POWER

In the history of African Americans in this country, there have been some tremendous movements and images that seem to capture the mood of the country and the black community at that time. And this one phrase "black power" is without a doubt one of the most simple and elegant statements of pride and unity in the black community. But it was also a phrase that came to represent the more violent and objectionable side of the struggle for equality in the black community. And that makes it a controversial phrase then and now.

Probably the greatest image of black power is the strong hand of a black man, clenched in a black glove and raised in the air in defiance and pride. Never has that salute been used so perfectly as it was at the 1968 Olympics when Tommy Smith and John Carlos raised the black power fist complete with black glove as they received their medals for their performances at those Olympic Games.

The phrase "Black Power" was not coined in a march or riot as might be implied. It was actually created by Robert Williams, the head of the NAACP in the early sixties. But it really started becoming a "street term" when it was adopted by Makasa Dada and Stokely Carmichael, founders of The Student Nonviolent Coordinating Committee which was the precursor to the famous Black Panther Party.

Sadly the black power movement became characterized by radical elements that went much further than seeking the goals of Martin Luther King and the rest of the civil rights movement's leadership. These radical elements sought black separation and social change by violent means. And so in a time when there was tremendous turmoil in the country because of the violence in Vietnam and on the streets of America because of that social strife, The Black Panthers and other fringe groups sewed fear and hatred in response to racism which at times made it more difficult to achieve long lasting change.

But there is good to be seen even in some of the darker elements of black history and the leadership who looked to find the best way forward for African Americans. Sometimes it is necessary for the radical elements to make themselves known so reasonable members of a community can know the outer limits and find compromise. This was a value to the black power movement because it did charge the discussion, albeit with violence and made the importance of reason- able Americans to come together to seek peaceful change all the more important.

But there is another good that came from the black power movement. Those images of the raised fist were images of a pride and a willingness to stand up for the rights of black Americans. They inspired a generation of young people to become more politically active, to stand up in their own world and make that statement made famous by James Brown *"Say it Loud. I'm Black and I'm Proud."*

That pride is an important thing and for young people to find. They have to find it in their communities and in their heroes. So if black youth took pride and courage to face their own circumstances from the bold stance of leaders who, albeit radically, said loud that black America was now going to be a force to be reckoned with, the resultant call to action to the black community produced many more positives than negatives. The fringe voice does speak what is in people's hearts and by getting that anger and frustration out, it became part of the movement. That energy could be captured and used for good instead of evil. And the end result was a movement that was energized for change and to make life better for all of black America. And that was what everybody wanted.

SLAVERY

Not everything that has to make a mark on the history of African American people is on the surface a positive thing.

But we know that there some very terrible things that happened to the black population in America that are undeniably a big part of the history of a people. So any survey of black history could not be complete without a discussion of slavery.

Few peoples of the earth have such a profoundly humiliating event to become such a central part of their heritage and their past. Yes, other tribes and races have endured slavery including the American Indian and the ancient Hebrews. Perhaps slavery is even more pivotal to the psychology of the African American culture because it is the central historical event that launched their start as citizens of this country.

It was not a citizenship born in nobility and honor as many others can point to in America. No to come to America as slaves is to have come to America with little more value to their fellow Americans than common livestock. And to be sure, the lives of slaves in the first decades of American history were very harsh times. Slaves were abused and denied anything that we might call today even basic human rights.

It is hard to gain any perspective on such a heinous crime against humanity as slavery except to put in context that this barbaric practice did not originate in America but came to our shores as part of the background of many people including the Dutch, the French and the English.

In some ways slavery was an evolution of the system of indentured servant hood in which an immigrant trades a certain number of years of service to a master in exchange for payment for their travel costs to come to America. But in the case of Africans who were brought on ships as slaves, there was no desire to come in chains to serve as property until death.

The impossibility of hope in that situation is almost impossible for any of us, black or white, in modern day

America to grasp or appreciate. But the efforts of slaves to free themselves and indeed to eventually do so using the Underground Railroad or other means is a testament to human will and that hope is something that is extremely hard to crush out in the human heart.

Has anything good come out of the legacy of slavery in this country? Well, a bond that was formed in the hearts of a people was permanently cemented during those horrible years. The music that the slaves used to keep their spirits alive has been passed to us as a rich legacy of spirituals that we cherish because they were born under inhumane suffering.

One thing that was a permanent out come of slavery in the African American community was the sense of resolve to never go back to such a time and a fight that was burned deep into the soul of a people to fight no matter how long or how hard to gain the civil rights of full citizens in this country. This would not have happened so profoundly had the peoples who came here and were identified solely by skin color not have endured slavery together. Before the various peoples who became slaves were pressed into service, they were from many tribes and many people all across Africa and beyond. Their nationalities were tribal and they had the normal pride of a people, customs, family relationships and history that any people will have.

That all was ripped away when they were taken into slavery.

But in the void left by those crucial relationships, a new brother- hood of African Americans was born. And the pride that has risen up in this new nation is strong and has continued to build throughout the decades. It is built on proud history and proud leadership. There has been much struggle and many difficulties and everything is not perfect by any measure. But the African American people can be proud of how far the culture has come and use that pride to press on toward greater accomplishments in the future.

THE UNDERGROUND RAILROAD

Sometimes when a people are under their most oppression that is when they truly are at their best it seems. And that adage could certainly be applied to those who operated the Underground Railroad in the 19th century while slavery was still the law of the land inAmerica.

The Underground Railroad was a means by which literally tens of thousands of slaves were able to escape their oppressors and make their way north to free states and a chance for freedom. It was so secretive that even to speak of it meant discovery and terrible punishment. But worse that that if it had been discovered by those who would stop slaves from finding their way out, it would have meant the end of hope for thousands of African Americans who were enduring the injustice of slavery.

The term "The Underground Railroad" was itself a code because that actual mechanism for moving slaves to freedom was not a rail- road at all. It was a series of stops, connected by obscure routes that wound their way through the countryside. The routes were twisted and illogical so those seeking to catch slaves and return them to bondage would be hard pressed to figure out the ways those seeking freedom might travel.

There was no published route for the Underground Railroad. "Passengers" made their way from safe house to safe house taking refuge in homes, churches and other out of the way locations that became known as "stations" to those in the know. Very often, the people who ran the stations along the path had no idea how long the railroad was or anything about the whole route. They simply knew enough to receive their "passengers", do all they could for their health and care and send them along with instructions on how to reach the next station.

The routes were treacherous and difficult. Slaves trying to reach freedom usually walked the routes from station to station to avoid public gathering places where slave chasers might find them and send them back to their owners in the south. And just as there was no real "railroad" to the Underground Railroad, the routes themselves were not actually under the ground. However many times at the safe houses, the owners will secure their guests in tunnels under the house or under a farm building.

At one such safe house in Nebraska City, Nebraska, there is a tunnel from the house to the barn so that if the farmer was feeding a needy family, they could quickly "disappear" if slave hunters arrived without notice. There were also roughly dug out bedrooms and crude accommodations under those houses to provide as much comfort and opportunities to rest and recover as was humanly possible under such difficult conditions.

We cannot leave our consideration of this phenomenal network without recognizing the courage of those who ran the "stations" to take in slaves, harbor them, feed them and care for their needs and help them along the way to try to do what they could to strike back at this inhuman practice of human slavery. It is a testimony to humanity that people would overcome their prejudices and reach out to strangers, putting their own homes and families at risk to help a downtrodden people in their time of great need.

And we must take a solemn moment and look back on a dark time in American and Black history when such measures were necessary. But the Underground Railroad spoke loudly that real Americans would not sit idly by and watch their fellow man suffer unjustly. There is no doubt that tens of thousands of lives were saved by these anonymous heroes who didn't do it for reward or recognition. They did it because it was the right thing to do and the thing God would expect them to do. It is an inspiration to us all in this day to lay down our own prejudices and bond together as brothers to resist prejudice, bigotry and mans cruelty to man because of these evils. If we do that we will know in our hearts, like those slaves on the railroad and the station owners knew, that there would come a better day.

THE DRED SCOTT DECISION

Not every significant event in the timeline of black history is a victory. In fact, many of the huge setbacks for African Americans in this country were the result of some very bad events that hurt the cause of civil liberties for Blacks for a long time. Such is the case in the infamous Dred Scott Decision.

It is important to get the context of why the Dred Scott case is so significant and to understand the facts of the case so we can be truly informed citizens. Dred Scott was a slave during that dark time in our history when slavery was legal. But the difference was that his owner took Dred Scott with him in a move to Wisconsin which was a free state where Scott lived in that legal status for many years. The movement on behalf of Dred's owner was because of military orders.

None of this was itself unusual until the master was again relocated to Missouri, a slave state and then the master passed away. The result was that Dred Scott's legal status was in question because he had spent so many years so recently as a resident of a free state. Abolitionists and others opposing slavery rallied to Dred Scott's defense and the case went all the way to the Supreme Court.

It was at the Supreme Court level that the decision was handed down that inflamed the divide between North and South in this country. The court decided that because of Scott's slave status, he was never and could never be a citizen of the United States and therefore had no standing in the eyes of the law. Hence he was trapped in his slave status despite his most recent residency.

This was a huge slap in the face to every free state in the union because it essentially nullified their status as a free state entirely. The court went on to make some truly astounding rulings related to the Dred Scott Case dictating that that Congress had no authority to keep slavery from coming about in new territories or states coming into the union and even declaring The Missouri Compromise which set in place the border between North and South to be unconstitutional.

This case set off such a wave of social and political repercussions that it could be considered to be a powder keg that set off the Civil War leading to the defeat of the south and the fall of slavery in America forever. Abraham Lincoln vehemently opposed the Dred Scott decision and spoke passionately against it only deepening the divide and the inevitability of war in America.

The lessons of the Dred Scott Case are many. For one thing it showed that even our revered Supreme Court which we count on for ultimate wisdom in all things ethical and legal, can be flawed in their judgment. No Supreme Court justice today would deny that these decisions were deeply flawed and failed to recognize the ultimate immorality of slavery or the fundamental denial of human rights to slaves that was guaranteed by our constitution.

But looking at the Dred Scott case in context, one wonders if it took such a dramatically upsetting ruling to put the wheels in motion to finally bring change to this country. There is no question that the Civil War was a bloody and horrible part of our national past. But the outcome of ending slavery forever was a fundamental need for this free society to continue to grow. Dred Scott had its place in that drama and in a strange way, we can be grateful it happened because of the outcome. It is very sad to see that it takes something so awful to make good come. But that was true in pre-Civil War days and, sadly, it is still true today.

THE HARLEM RENAISSANCE

The quest for equality and freedom for African Americans has been fought on many fronts. But there is no question that in the area of the arts, the contribution of black America has been so profound that it has greatly eased racial tensions and changed the image of black culture profoundly in the eyes of all Americans. Many have criticized the world of such black performers as Richard Prior, Bill Cosby and Eddie Murphy but these artists along with artists in literature, painting, poetry, music and all the arts have brought an acceptance of black culture that has furthered the appreciation of African Americans by all people more than anything else ever could do.

In the history of black culture, the Harlem Renaissance in the 1920s was a time when African American culture truly was showcased for the country, indeed the world and people started to realize the rich legacy that was available to all peoples in black culture. The Harlem Renaissance was more than just a greater exposure to black dance, music, comedy or theater even though the chance for all peoples to appreciate the talents of black artists was certainly worthwhile in its own right.

But the Harlem Renaissance also refers to the cultural and social movements of the time in which black pride was beginning to cause big changes in the way African Americans thought about themselves and eventually how all Americans thought of black Americans as well. A lot of factors led to the explosion of black culture during that time frame especially in New York City. The city had been a Mecca for artists of every culture for a long time as it still is today. And during this time frame there was a migration of the African American population to the north and to the urban industrial areas particularly to take advantage of the economic opportunities there.

With the migration of the African American population came the rich black music that had continued to grow and evolve ever since the Civil War. But because of the concentration of cultures in New York and the willingness to experiment, to blend and to discover new cultures that was the norm in that melting pot city, white America too began to discover the jazz, blues, spirituals and gospel music that began to evolve and integrate into many secular musical styles of the time.

The era was in every way a renaissance just as much as the great cultural renaissance in Europe had been many years before it. In every genre, black culture exploded onto the national consciousness. Many outstanding, stand-out names that became household names for literature and the arts came into their own during the Harlem Renaissance including Langston Hughes, Booker T. Washington, Louis Armstrong, Duke Ellington and Jelly Roll Morton.

There is no question that the cultural explosion that occurred during that brief time frame created a tidal wave of change that is still being felt today. The blending of blues, gospel and spirituals, when it began to see experimentation by the likes of Elvis Presley, Jerry Lee Lewis and Little Richard spawned and even bigger cultural event known as rock and roll music that changed the world forever. And to this day many of the mannerisms, the approach to style and speech that came to be known as "being cool" was in reality an attempt, especially by youth, to emulate black culture.

And by imitation cultures began to merge and blend to where they could never live separately again. And that blending and enjoyment of black culture has done much to help integrate society and make social change and acceptance of each other's cultures by black and white a possibility today.

BOOKER T. WASHINGTON

As you travel this great nation, it is no accident you will see a lot of schools given the name of Booker T. Washington. That is because this great black educator and leader set the standard and carved out a new path in the years right after the fall of slavery to lead his people to a better way. He showed his people a way of education, accomplishment, achievement and the prosperity that naturally comes with those goals.

In 1901, the biography of Booker T. Washington was published with the fitting title "Up From Slavery." Washington's struggle to rise up from the limitations of a slave's life to be come one of the most respected black leaders in America is one of the reasons he is revered in black history as one of the greats who really made a difference for his people.

When Booker T. Washington's family was freed from slavery in Virginia, young Booker immediately began pursuing the path where he would make his mark, in education. Achieving success at Hampton University and then at Wayland Seminary, he was soon to pioneer new achievements for African Americans in higher education, becoming one of the first leaders of the Tuskegee University in Alabama.

But it was more than just academic success that marked Washing- ton's career. He became prominent in many areas of leadership becoming a spokesperson for post slavery black America to the powerful and influential in this country. Book T. Washington lived the concept that the pen was mightier than the sword and was an early voice for moderation and learning to excel within the institutions and customs of America rather than deal in violence.

One of Washington's great strengths was finding partnership and coalitions between leaders of many communities to improve the opportunities for education and excellence for the African American community of the time. One of the most influential speeches of black history was given by Washington and became known as the Atlanta Address of 1895 in which Washington, speaking to a largely white audience instigated a profound change in way economic opportunity and hiring was done in America at its time. In that one speech he...

Called up on the black community to become part of the economy and industry of America thus beginning the healing process that was so necessary at the time.

Stated without reservation that the south was the region of the country where there were the greatest opportunities for black employment. By bringing together the strong black labor force with an economy in the midst of recovery from the civil war, Washington may have been one of the chief architects for the recovery of the south from the ravages of that war.

Introduced to the economic institutions predominantly run by the white citizens of the country that it made more sense to take advantage of the large resident black population for reliable workers than to look to immigrants. The outcome was a boom in employment for the black community that was a huge leap forward in the struggle to rise up out of slavery.

The Atlanta Address of 1895 propelled Booker T. Washington into national prominence becoming a healing voice and a powerful catalyst for change in this country. Using his sophisticated network of supporters from every arena of leadership including political, academic and business leaders, Washington worked tirelessly to provide hope and new opportunities for black families trying to make their way in America.

His work ethic was profound and produced change at a rate that was phenomenal by any standard. But it took a toll on Washington who died relatively young, at the age of 59 from exhaustion and over- work. But this too points out the tremendous drive and devotion this important black leader had to use all of his talents, his intellect and his contacts to better the lives of black people and speed the road to acceptance and integration across America. We all owe a Booker T. Washington a great deal of gratitude for being "the man of the hour" to lead all people forward, black and white, to find ways to work together in partnership rather than with distrust or violence to achieve a better America for everyone.

GEORGE WASHINGTON CARVER

There is leadership that talks and there is leadership that works and in the hall of fame of great black leaders over the decades, George Washington Carver was a leader that worked. His leadership was not the kind that tried to capture publicity or make great fame for himself. He didn't try to start a movement or achieve change through violence or confrontation, although those things are sometimes necessary.

Instead, George Washington Carver showed leadership by making contributions to the welfare of his people that would last a lifetime. His selfless spirit is an inspiration to all peoples of any race, creed or color.

He is probably best known for his discoveries in the use of the peanut. And while it's true that Carver was credited with over 300 discoveries to find new uses for the common peanut, his innovations did not end there. He continued his research to find important uses for other common agricultural products such as the sweet potato, pecans and soybeans.

George Washington Carver truly took the hands of his people where they were at the time and lead them forward to a better life. And where the black community was in the nineteenth century was agriculture. This was where a black family looked for their food, their living and their opportunity to better themselves. And that is what George Washington Carver made possible.

He was in every way a self made man, setting out at a young age to attain a better education for himself, he set an example to all that education was the path to freedom for his people and for all people. He truly had to struggle to achieve his success as he worked his way up through high school and then at Simpson Collage in Iowa where he was the first and only black student and then on to Iowa Agricultural College.

His success at Iowa Agricultural College came from determination and his ability to use his natural genius to succeed against all odds. But his breakthroughs were nothing short of revolutionary introducing such ideas as crop rotation to southern agriculture that revolutionized how farming could be done and gave his people the chance to become genuinely profitable in their daily work.

As he found success in his private career, he never used his discoveries to gather wealth of fame for himself. Instead he wanted his work to benefit his people and all of mankind. He was quotes as saying concerning his talents, "God gave them to me. How can I sell them to someone else?"

These were not just idle words that he spoke because he lived that philosophy evidenced by when he donated his life savings to start the Carver Research Foundation at Tuskegee to make sure that an institution existed to continue his important work in agriculture. Small wonder that the fitting remembrance that was etched on his grave read "He could have added fortune to fame, but caring for neither, he found happiness and honor in being helpful to the world."

The legacy of George Washington Carver would be one that set the standard high for black leadership in decades to come. It was a legacy of servant leadership, of concern for his people and for making genuine contributions to improving what was really important, the living standard and well being for all African

Americans, not just the fortunate few. He is truly an inspiration for all of us who look at the struggle the black community has endured over the centuries and a figure to celebrate as a bright and shining leader in black history.

HARRIET TUBMAN

Sometimes when we think of legionary outlaws who gave their life efforts to help a downtrodden and oppressed people, figures like Robin Hood or some other dashing male hero springs to mind. In black history, we have just such a character but this champion of her people did not ride the forests with merry men. Harriet Tubman, a humble and diminutive black woman truly qualifies as such a profoundly legendary figure that her exploits would rival Robin Hood's or any other hero of cultural legend. Small wonder she was often referred to as "Moses of her People."

Harriet Tubman was born in 1822 in Dorchester County, Maryland to a slave family of the estate of Anthony Thompson. During her slave years, she endured many hardships and harsh treatment which left her with scars and even as susceptibility to epileptic seizures that resulted from a head injury. It was common for slaves to change hands and that was part of Harriet's life as well. Finally in 1849, she ran away to freedom but she by far did not run away from her people.

Over the next few years, Harriet Tubman became a true warrior for the salvation of her people who were locked in slavery. Harriet didn't just find a safe place and count her blessings for making it to free- dom. She saw the need for the Underground Railroad in the salvation of hundreds more like her and it became her life's mission to maintain the regional stations of that railroad for as long as it took to give liberty to all who had the courage to flee slavery via that resource.

Harriet Tubman showed the kind of courage, resourcefulness and intellect that a field general for any army would be proud to boast. All totaled Tubman lead thirteen separate missions to bring African Americans to freedom along the Underground Railroad. That means that she personally lead over seventy slaves to freedom and had a direct influence on the freeing of at least that many more. And by keeping the Underground Railroad operational and out of the reach of slave hunters and authorities who sought to shut it down, she indirectly was influential in the salvation of hundreds, perhaps thou- sands more. Who can say how many prosperous and influential black families in this country today owe the lives of their ancestors and the success they have achieved since those dark days to the brave work of Harriet Tubman.

When the Civil War occurred, Harriet didn't retire satisfied that she had done her work for her people. She continued to work tirelessly for abolitionist movements and to do her part for the war effort. She became one of the first ever female spies for the North during the war and her military abilities were so well developed that she actually was put in a position of leadership to command the raid on Combahee Ferry in 1863.

After the Civil War was over, Harriet Tubman continued her work on behalf of abolitionist movements and for women's rights until she retired to write her memoirs. Her contribution during this crucial time in black history was so revered that the US Postal Service honored her with a stamp in 1978.

There have been many heroes and heroines in the long uphill struggle for liberation, freedom and equality for African Americans in this country. During this brutal time when Harriet Tubman stood in the gap for her people, the plight of black Americans was as much life and death as any other time in history. Small wonder her name is revered as one of the icons of the fight for freedom prior to the Civil War. And small wonder she was referred to as Moses to Her People and will be remembered in that way for generations to come.

THE TRIUMPH AT THE BERLIN OLYMPICS

There have been many truly memorable moments in black history where the blatant wrongness of racial discrimination has been dramatically put on display. The 1936 Olympics in Hitler's Germany may be one of the most dramatic because of what the madman wanted to happen and what really happened.

Hitler was pleased to host the Olympics because he felt it was a chance to put on display one of his core philosophical concepts which was the superiority of the Aryan race. Or to put it more bluntly, Hitler wanted to show the superiority of the white man on the Olympic fields. Looking back on his arrogance, and knowing what we do today, you wonder how he could have been so deeply wrong about something. But if he had never questioned that theory, he should have given it serious review after the Berlin Olympics.

Once again, it was a man whose name in black history has become one of great pride that turned the day for justice and equality. That man was Jessie Owens who came to those Olympics not to make a racial statement or start a movement but to do his best and show his pride as a black man, as an American and as an athlete. And that pride shown through as he won four gold metals and turned Hitler's hopes for an Aryan romp over the black man to dust.

Hitler's response was infantile and nauseating storming out of the stadium as Owens won event after event and then refusing to shake Jessie's hand when the time to award the metals came. But there is another side to this story that sheds another light on where we were in black history at that time. And that was the experience Jesse Owens had in Germany from the other athletes and from the German citizens who were warm and welcoming to him and treated him as the athletic hero he was as a result of his great accomplishments.

History tells us that during the long jump competition, Jesse's German competitor, Lutz Long, gave him advice and was friendly throughout the competition. As he continued to put on display his remarkable athletic ability, the German citizens, some 110,000 strong cheered him enthusiastically and eagerly asked him for his auto- graph when he was on the streets after the competition. In fact, Owens enjoyed equality that is common among athletes as he traveled with his fellow white athletes, ate with them and stayed in the same living accommodations with them, something that would have been out of the question in America at the time.

There are many lessons we can gather from Jesse's experience beyond that obvious that Hitler's ideas of Aryan supremacy were deeply wrong and offensive to all mankind, not just to the victims of discrimination. We see that even in a society that has become characterized as racist, such as Germany in the 1930's, the people, the common everyday folk of Germany had no room in their hearts for such racism that was being pushed upon them by their leadership. This can be a source of inspiration and hope for all of us and an encouragement not to prejudge a people who we might even perceive as being racists because many times the good people, the common everyday people will have nothing to do with such evil.

And we can celebrate this great victory in a very difficult circumstance in which it wasn't speeches that proved that race or color or creed don't make a man superior. Instead it is the talent, the integrity and the hard work of each individual that shows the quality that is from within. Jesse Owens demonstrated that even to the likes of Adolph Hitler. And we have that opportunity to demonstrate that same principle every day in our daily lives.

JACKIE ROBINSON

There are a lot of "firsts" in the long history of African Americans in this country. And with each one, a new plateau

of equality and acceptance was achieved. But it can also be said without exception that each one came at a price for the brave people who fought hard to improve the lives of their people and achieve that great breakthrough in their chosen field.

These principles are certainly true in the arena of sports and especially baseball. Baseball has long been considered the great American pastime. So on April 15th, 1947 when Jackie Robinson walked out onto the field to be the first black to shatter the color barrier in professional baseball in a game between his team, the

Brooklyn Dodgers and the Boston Braves, he was making a dramatic statement.

But this was no day of parades and celebration for Robinson. As is the case in so many great events in black history, that was time of tremendous racism, prejudice and discrimination against African Americans. Jackie Robinson was an extraordinary baseball player. In his first year alone he played 151 games, led the league in his base stealing ability and was awarded with the first rookie of the year award ever given. While Jackie played with the Dodgers, they went to the World Series six times and he played in six all star games as well. He was a solid performer and a tremendous benefit to his team for which he won the most valuable player award in 1949 and helped the Dodgers win the World Series in 1955.

As is often the case, it took some brave leadership from supporters outside of the African American community to see to it that prejudice would not keep a brilliant career such as Jackie Robinsons from reaching its true potential. When some of the Brooklyn Dodger players refused to sit next to Jackie Robinson and showed other hostile attitudes towards him because of his race, management stood firm that if they could not become a team with all members of the club, they were welcome to go play baseball elsewhere.

But one of the most emotional and heart warming moments that has become a shining example of the fall of racial bigotry in this country came in a game in Cincinnati Ohio in Robinson's rookie year. As the fans at the game began to heckle and shout racial slurs at Robinson, one of his fellow Dodger's, Pee Wee Reese, took a stand to bring this kind of behavior to a stop. His statement that racism would no longer rule in baseball was simple and elegant. As fans shouted their hateful remarks, Reese walked out on the field and put his arm around Jackie Robinson clearly communicating that this man was a teammate and a valued ball player on that team. The taunts ended abruptly and Reese and Robinson went on to do what they came to that game to do, play outstanding baseball.

Jackie himself never made his baseball career about race. He chose to demonstrate dramatically what Dr. Martin Luther King later described when he said that the day must come when we judge a man not by the color of his skin but by the content of his character.

Jackie Robinson made his stand for equality by showing that at the heart of his character was a superior baseball player and a valued member of the baseball community.

Even when Robinson spoke of his days pioneering

baseball for other African Americans, his words demonstrated that he only wanted the chance to be tested fairly alongside all other athletes, no more and no less. His simple statements really summarized so much of what the civil rights movement was all about when he said, "You can hate a man for many reasons, color is not one of them." And later in his career he stated it again beautifully when he said, "I'm not concerned with your liking or disliking me... all I ask is that you respect me as a human being."

This emphasis on the individual, on the quality of all men and all Americans and their right to be judged for who they are as people, not subjected to prejudice as African Americans is a perfect summation of the struggle of African Americans everywhere.

A TROUBLED TIME

From 1955 to 1965 there was a war right in the middle of America. No, it wasn't a war like World War II or the Revolutionary War.

It was a war for the heart and soul of this country to determine once and for all if America was really going to be a land of equal opportunity for all. It is a war that eventually took on the name of "The Civil Rights Movement."

Make no mistake, this was not just a shouting match. Some of the events that we even remember today became quite brutal and deadly. Those who fought in this war on both sides were deadly serious about the causes they represented and willing to fight and even die to see their cause succeed. The war waged for years and steady progress was made but not without tremendous sacrifice by the leaders of the movement who were committed to a giving a new meaning to the phrase "set my people free."

In all of black history, there may be no more significant a time since the Civil War when the rights of African Americans were so deeply fought and won. The tensions in the country had been build- ing. When the Supreme Court mandated desegregation in the schools in the historic case Brown versus the Board of Education, the stage was set. But it was on December 1, 1955 when Rosa Parks refused to give up her seat on a bus in Montgomery, Alabama to a white man that the movement finally took shape and became a titanic struggle for the rights of African Americans in America. That first battle brought to the front line one of the most important figures to fight for Civil Rights of that era, the Reverend Martin Luther King.

This tremendous struggle for freedom was never easy and was often marked with violence. Over the next ten years some of the most important milestone in black history took place:

1957 – President Eisenhower had to send federal troops to Arkansas to secure admission to Central High School by nine black students.

1960 – The sit-in at Woolworths lunch counter in

Greensboro North Carolina set the stage for nonviolent protest that was used with great success for the rest of the struggle. Nonviolent protest and civil disobedience became a staple of the civil rights movement because of the influence of Martin Luther King.

1963 – The historic March on Washington in which over 200,000 people gathered to hear Dr. Kings famous "I Have a Dream" speech.

1964 – President Lyndon Johnson signed the bill that was the most significant event of his presidency and one he believed deeply in, the Civil Rights Act of 1964.

1965 – The assignation of Malcolm X and the Watts race rights.

1965 – President Johnson takes another bold step to accelerate the civil rights movement implementing Affirmative Action when he issues Executive Order 11246.

This short list is just a few of the highlights of this troubled time in which the rights of all citizens of American, black and white and of all colors were being redefined both on the streets, in the courts and in the different branches of government. In the years to come there would be great steps forward. One by one, every area of American life would see breakthroughs by African Americans in the areas of sports, entertainment, education and politics. There were many proud moments and there were moments of tremendous shame and heinous acts committed by both white and black people. But through all that struggle, the society continued to grow and adapt to the will of the people as has always been the tradition in American culture.

The struggle is far from over. Discrimination and hate speech continue to be a problem to this day. And while it is easy to reflect on those days of struggle with regret, we can also look at them with pride. We can be proud of the great leaders who demonstrated tremendous courage and wisdom to lead this nation to a better way of life. And we can be proud of America because it is here where such a struggle can result in equality and freedom for all citizens, not just a few.

AFFIRMATIVE ACTION

The history of the growth of equality for African Americans in America has been one of great accomplishments followed by many small gains and many setbacks as well. The outlawing of slavery did not instantly make all blacks equal with whites in America. It took many subsequent legal actions as well as hundreds of social efforts, big and small, to slowly make the progress we have seen today. But even in this day and age, in a new century, there is an ongoing battle against racism. It seems we need leadership to guide society to true equality as much now as ever in our history.

The abolition of slavery only began the long hard struggle for African American culture to become a true part of what it means to be an American. That is because even though the legal definition of slavery had been thrown down, the attitudes and cultural systems in place to keep the races separate and to deny black people rights equal with whites had to be addressed one by one.

Slowly over the decades, we have seen big changes but many came at a great cost. From the legal granting of the right to vote to African Americans to the civil rights movement to school desegregation, each step forward came with resistance, great difficulty and significant sacrifice from leaders and ordinary citizens alike to make each step toward true equality a fact.

Of all the efforts to "level the playing field", none has been more controversial than the Affirmative Action program. In its beginning, it was intended to be a supplement to the Civil Rights Act of 1964. Over time it had become clear that despite removal of laws that enforced segregation or discrimination, there seemed to be a natural segregation in the work place that was keeping African Americans from getting a fair chance at jobs because of the prejudices of an employer, even if that prejudice was not officially recognized in the company charter.

There were two significant executive orders that made affirmative action a reality. The first was Executive Order 10925 signed by President Kennedy on March

6, 1965 which was the first law to make mention of the phrase. This was followed by much more sweeping Civil Rights Act which was signed into law by President Johnson. Together these laws attempted to correct by legal means the disparity of opportunity that existed in the workplace for people of color by instituting a system of quotas that employers had to meet to satisfy federal affirmative action minority employment levels.

But as often is the case when the government attempts to impose right attitudes via legislation, these laws often created as many problems for minorities as they cured. Nevertheless as the application of the quota systems began to become widespread, it did open many doors for African Americans that would not have opened due to racial prejudice and silent segregation that was keeping the African American community from reaching its economic potential.

In truth, nobody really liked this kind of imposed fairness system. For whites, they felt the sting of an artificial system of judgment that was sometimes called "reverse discrimination". While there was some justice that the white community got a taste for what it felt like to lose out on opportunity due to the color of your skin, it did not help the country in our goal of growing together to become one "color blind" community.

Affirmative action is a mixed blessing for the African American community. While it did its job in the short term to opening doors that were closed due to racism, it is not the ideal solution. That is because it did not fulfill Dr. King's vision of a world where a man is judged not by the color of his skin but by the content of his character. We can hope that we will grow to that point as a culture and look back on affirmative action as an unfortunate but necessary provision to help us grow and mature as a truly integrated culture.

BROWN VERSUS THE BOARD OF EDUCATION

In 1951, thirteen families in the small community of Topeka, Kansas got together to do something about an unjust situation. The board of education of their community was allowing racial segregation in the school system based on an out of date 1879 law. The leader of this group of concerned parents was Oliver J. Brown and the outcome of what started out as a few parents trying to make life better for their children became one of the most infamous and influential supreme court cases in history known as Brown versus the Board of Education.

The practice of school segregation had become a common and accepted practice in American society despite many movements in the history of civil rights to stop the separation of black society from white. The justification that segregation provided a "separate but equal" setting which benefited education, the truth was it was a thinly veiled attempt to deprive African American children of the quality of education that all people need to excel in the modern world.

The case continued to gather momentum until it came before the Supreme Court in May of 1954. The decision was stunning and decisive when it came back 9-0. The statement of the court was brief, eloquent and to the point stating that "separate educational facilities are inherently unequal."

Now even such a definitive statement from the Supreme Court did not end the struggle between segregationists and those who would end the practice that deprived African American children of quality education. In 1957 the Arkansas governor tried to block the integration of schools in his state and the only thing that could stop him was the intervention of federal troops sent by President Eisenhower. A similar but much more well publicized event occurred in Alabama where Governor George Wallace physically blocked black students from entering the University of Alabama. It took the intervention of federal marshals to physically remove him to assure that the law of the land, as mandated by The Supreme Court, was carried out. And the law of the land then and forever since then was that segregation was illegal in this country.

Since this landmark decision, there have been other more crafty attempts to resurrect segregation. But over the decades, attitudes have shifted to where such views on how our social institutions are set up are considered old fashioned and uneducated.

The integration of the schools was an important step in the ongoing struggle to create a truly equal society and to improve the chances of black children to grow up with the same opportunities as all other children in this country. As more and more African American children became well educated, the black population has been able to make a strong contribution to the culture and to the advancement of knowledge in every discipline of learning. Further, the growing educated black population brought about the black middle class which equalized society from an economic point of view. As African Americans began to participate in all of the economic opportunities that middle class prosperity afforded them, the chances for whites, blacks and people of all races and cultures to mix has been healthy to heal the scars of racism and slowly erase divisions in the culture.

But maybe the most important outcome of integration of the schools is the opportunity it has given for children of all races to learn, play and grow together. As young black and white students have attended classes, gone to football games and hung out at pep rallies together, they have become friends. They have had chances to work together on teams and socialize under many situations and as that has become the social norm, racism began to evaporate from the hearts of young America.

As a result, youth of modern times look on racism as a strange and primitive viewpoint from long ago and not in step with an up to date view of the world. This kind of true acceptance both by whites toward blacks and by blacks toward whites will go further to finally end racial separation and intolerance more than any riot or protest or march or even ruling from the Supreme Court could ever do. And we have Oliver Brown and that small group of parents from Topeka, Kansas to thank for this. By doing what was best for their kids, they did something wonderful for all of America's children both now and for generations to come.

ROSA PARKS

In any great movement which affects great change in a nation or a people, there is something called a watershed moment. A water- shed moment is that one signature event that triggered the onslaught of great and historic change. In American history, that watershed moment might be the Boston Tea Party. But in the context of black history, particularly when we consider the central role that the civil rights movement has played in black history in this country, there is really just one watershed moment that virtually anybody who understands black history will point to.

That event that took place on December 1, 1955 on a simple city bus when a black woman by the name of Rosa Parks got on that bus. When the bus became crowded, the bus driver ordered Ms. Parks to relinquish her seat to a white man as was the cultural order of things at that time. But Rosa Parks was not interested in seeing that cultural order of things continue. She refused to give up that seat.

The explosion of outrage and social change that was released by that one simple act of civil disobedience is the watershed moment that anyone affected by the civil rights movement points to at the most important event in modern black history. Rosa Parks was arrested for not giving her seat up that day and the trial for that act of civil disobedience brought to the national spotlight another important leader in the civil rights movement by the name of Dr. Martin Luther King, Jr.

This one event began to escalate and gather energy in the black community. It was an exciting and somewhat frightening time as the black community was energized and began to organize around these two courageous leaders and the result was the most powerful civil rights protests in the history of the movement occurred which came to be known as the Montgomery Bus Boycott.

There are many reasons why such a simple event has had such a powerful effect on a people such as it did on the black community of the fifties. Clearly the frustration and gathering power of a movement was already building in the black community. A situation like this can best be described as a tinderbox that is just waiting for a spark for it to explode into fire. When that simple black woman finally decided that she was no longer going to live in servitude to the white man and she put her foot down and said NO, which was the spark that set the civil rights movement in motion.

Rosa Parks was not a trained instigator or a skilled manipulator of groups. Because she was just a citizen and a simple woman with simple daily needs, that itself was a powerful statement that this was the time for the community to take action and affect change. She was not even looking to start a nation changing civil rights movement when she refused to give up her bus seat. As she said later in an inter- view about the event..."I would have to know for once and for all what rights I had as a human being and a citizen of Montgomery, Alabama." And then in her autobiography, My Story she elaborated that... "People always say that I didn't give up my seat because I was tired, but that isn't true. I was not tired physically, or no more tired than I usually was at the end of a working day. I was not old, although some people have an image of me as being old then. I was forty-two. No, the only tired I was, was tired of giving in."

Rosa Parks won the right to be treated as a human being for herself and for her people across America and even around the world with her simple act of civil disobedience. She is an inspiration to us all that we too must demand the right of simple human dignity for all people who are citizens of this great land. And the story of Rosa Park's defiance shows that if we demand that, it will be won.

MARTIN LUTHER KING, JR.

When you sit back and take in the phenomenal achievements of black history, it is natural to be moved to admiration by

some of the great figures of black history including Booker T. Washington, George Washington Carver and many more. But one name stands head and shoulders above the rest and that is the name Martin Luther King, Jr.

Dr. King's legacy of change and his call for the end of racism and segregation in American society is without question the voice that has moved America as no other has done. For while many have showed tremendous leadership, Dr. King clearly demonstrated a vision for the future of America in which black and white worked, lived, played and worshipped together as one society not two.

The honor and reverence all American's have for Martin Luther King, Jr. is evident in how honored his name has become since his tragic death at the assassins hand in 1968. All around this nation, virtually every U.S. city has named a major road after the great civil rights leader. He singularly has a U.S. holiday named after him, an honor usually reserved for presidents. He has been honored on the U.S. stamp and no school child gets through his or her elementary education without knowing the key phrases from Dr. King's famous "I have a dream" speech.

Dr. King's career in civil rights is inseparable from the early struggles of the civil rights movement from the late fifties going forward. Our images of him walking side by side with his people unifying them behind his leadership and facing tremendous hatred and racial bigotry to take a stand in America to say without compromise that racism would not stand in this country any more.

Those images of Dr. King working and marching with others who shared his courage to step out and make a change for the better are indelible on the American consciousness. For Dr. King was not a leader who sent his messages from the safety and comfort of a far away office. No, he was there, in the midst of his people, marching on Washington arm in arm with the everyday men and women of this country who banded together to fight the evils of racism. It took tremendous courage for Dr. King to take to the streets with his people like he did and it was a risk that eventually cost him his life. But his courage inspired thousands to be courageous too and be one people, one brotherhood who would no longer allow racism to be the rule of law in America.

Dr. King's famous speech from the steps of the Lincoln Memorial on a hot August 28, 1963 has become so central to our American heritage that it is quoted with reverence by scholars, students and all people seeking their own inspiration from this great man. This speech ranks with Kennedy's inaugural speech and the Lincoln's Gettysburg Address as words that have inspired this nation as none other have been able to do. It is impossible not to get goose bumps reading these key phrases from that historic speech.

I have a dream that one day this nation will rise up and live out the true meaning of its creed: 'We hold these truths to be self-evident, that all men are created equal.'"

"I have a dream that my four little children will one day live in a nation where they will not be judged by the color of their skin but by the content of their character."

"Let freedom ring. And when this happens, and when we allow freedom ring—when we let it ring from every village and every hamlet, from every state and every city, we will be able to speed up that day when all of God's children—black men and white men, Jews and Gentiles, Protestants and Catholics—will be able to join hands and sing in the words of the old Negro spiritual: "Free at last! Free at last! Thank God Almighty, we are free at last!"

When reading Dr. King's prophetic words to us all, his ideas become our ideas and we all become challenged to make his dream come to life. And that is what is truly the definition of a great leader.

MARTIN LUTHER KING JR.'S DREAM

In the history of any great people, sometimes there is a singular moment that so sums up that struggle and challenges the hearts

of the people of the time that this moment becomes one that is both historic and mythical. In the long history the African American in this country, one such singular moment was the delivery of what has come to be referred to as the "I have a dream" speech during the historic March on Washington in August of 1963.

There are many things about this speech that are so poetic that the text of the speech has become one of the great historic texts of the nation's history as well as of black history. That is why virtually any school child can recite the most stirring words from the speech which are...

And so even though we face the difficulties of today and tomorrow, I still have a dream. It is a dream deeply rooted in the American dream. I have a dream that one day this nation will rise up and live out the true meaning of its creed: "We hold these truths to be self-evident, that all men are created equal." I have a dream that my four little children will one day live in a nation where they will not be judged by the color of their skin but by the content of their character.

What is most striking about this text if you read the entire text is the hope. And it's a wonderful tradition for every family to read this speech, perhaps on Martin Luther's King's birthday which is now a national holiday. Dr. King called upon his people to look up and look with hope toward tomorrow. But more than that, he called on all people to work together toward a shared hope, a hope of fulfilling the American dream that he discusses with such passion in his words.

The setting for the speech was on the steps of the Lincoln memorial, within view of the Congress, the reflecting pool and the White House on the National Mall in the center Washington D.C. Dr. King called it hallowed ground reflecting his deep reference and respect for the icons of this country and his deep love of country which too comes through in the speech.

But it was a speech of struggle because he spoke of the fact that black people in America were still not living in an openly free and equal status with all other citizens. Dr King did not loose touch with the reality of the tough lives African Americans were living in the United States. That is why this speech is so perfectly crafted and so perfectly delivered. It combines the harsh reality and resolve by black leaders and the African American population to make the world better for themselves and their children with a hope and an optimism that this was a country that would not put up with the oppression and discrimination that has kept black people down ever since slavery.

It is a speech that issued a call to action in the time frame of "Now" which was a call to action that many in the houses of power in our country took heed. They did take action immediately to get the process of renewal and repair of a broken social system moving in the right direction. One of the outcomes of this speech was the historic Civil Rights Act of 1964 which changed the fabric of the country forever in the legal restrictions it put on discrimination in every aspect of American life.

If it had not been for the "I have a dream" speech, the March on Washington on that hot and humid August day might have just been another in the many protests and events of the civil rights era. Instead it became an iconic moment in American and black history that changed Dr. King into a national hero for black and white people alike and energized a movement and a nation to take matters into their own hands and make thing better for all people.

THURGOOD MARSHALL

In the long history of uphill struggle for blacks in America, there are many notable firsts. In addition black history is populated with some truly notable black heroes who made significant contributions to the prosperity of African Americans and the kind of change that brings about full citizenship and acceptance for African Americans at every tier of society. One such American hero was Thurgood Marshall.

The bare facts of the rise of this black leader don't say enough about the tremendous influence his work did to improve race relations in this country. Thurgood was the great grandson of a slave and his father did well to educate the boy in the value of education and of the law in modern society. His brilliant school career which culminated in graduating Magnum Cum Laud from Howard University was the launch of just a brilliant legal career.

Throughout his time as a lawyer, Marshall's success in arguing anti segregation and discrimination cases was phenomenal. As chief council for the NAACP, Marshall argued before the Supreme Court 29 times, winning each case he took on. Later when he served in the circuit court, he made 112 rulings that were all fully upheld by the Supreme Court.

But there can be no more phenomenal moment in the life of Thur- good Marshall or in black history itself as when in 1967, President Lyndon Johnson appointed Thurgood Marshall to the Supreme Court. This appointment represented a long uphill climb to see African American leaders take on significant roles of influence in the local, state and federal governments throughout America. For all of the violent social protests and struggles "on the streets" in the sixties and seventies lead by notable black leaders such as Martin Luther King and Malcolm X, it can be argued that the lasting influence Thurgood Marshall in his time on the Supreme Court made just as much impact to improve the lives of black Americans as any other leader of his time.

When you look at the time frame that Thurgood

Marshall demonstrated his leadership at a national level, this was a watershed time period in which he made great strides to take this country from one still being affected by the attitudes and social systems of slavery and a past full of discrimination to a society on a clear path to become a truly integrated society of the future.

There can really be no greater single accomplishment that Thurgood Marshall made than his victory in the Brown versus the Board of Education case. It was the success in the case that effectively brought school segregation to a halt once and for all in America. While there was still work to be done to make that legal reality one that was part of the lives of all Americans, Thurgood Marshall opened the door for all African Americans to find the same level of high educational excellence that he role modeled for black youth of his day. In doing so, the economic standard of living and educational level of black America rose significantly throughout his time on the bench giving rise to the first black middle class that only added to the movement of the integration of society across all tiers and situations.

It is for these many good reasons that we would include Thurgood Marshall among the truly great heroes of black history of the last one hundred years. His contribution to the court and the changes in the legal status of Blacks and all minorities and underprivileged people in this country has made America a better place to live for all. He has set a standard for future black leadership and indeed for all of us to live up to the best of our values to see to it that equality and justice for all persons in our society continues to be the rule of law in this country for a long time to come.

THE HALLS OF POWER

Black history has been a progressive climb from without the lowest echelons of society during slavery to the highest. When you think of black history, we often think of the civil rights movement, of John Brown's violent protests, of the Underground Railroad. But black history doesn't end with any one event. It is always in the process of being made every day.

Even in the last two decades, huge steps forward have been made at the very top governmental positions by notable and highly qualified black Americans who are making all of us proud in the contributions they are making to America. Colin Powell was an accomplished general who demonstrated with quiet dignity and authority that he could lead many men into battle. He was rewarded for his valiant efforts finally reaching the very top levels of the government serving as President

Bush's Secretary of State in his first administration. Throughout the halls of government and anywhere Secretary Powell served, he was treated with respect and the honor that he deserved for serving his country so well.

Following the honorable service of Colin Powell a just as distinguished public servant, a black woman by the name of Condoleezza Rice. It was a proud day when she stepped into that office showing how far America had come from the days when blacks could not eat in the same restaurants as whites or drink from the same drinking fountains. And her service has been just as distinguished, meeting with heads of state from Africa to Europe to the Middle East to South America and making great accomplishments throughout her career.

These two African Americans are true examples of Doctor King's vision of people who were recognized not for the color of their skin but the content of their character. Their excellence as leaders and their amazing resume's they brought to their jobs provide tremendous inspiration to black boys and girls in school that they too can rise up in this society and go as far as they want to go if they let their natural gifts and skills come to the surface. They do not need a government program or special help to succeed. America has far to go but Dr. Rice and General Powell are examples that the system can reward black people of excellence and will not overlook the contributions they can make to America's future.

And now we are on that part of black history that is yet to be. The future is a part of black history yet to be written. And we witness another black leader of excellence preparing to be considered for the very top position of power in the country, perhaps in the world, the presidency of the United States. And as with General Powell and Dr. Rice, Barrack Obama will not be judged as a black man or in the context of the racial struggle in this country. Already he is being admired and praised for his leadership, his eloquence and his ability to bring new vision to this country. It is a day of pride for all of black America to see Barrack Obama be considered for this position. He will have to work hard and be judged on his talents, skills, experience and ability to lead. But it's a testimony to how far the country has come that he has just as much of a chance to win that election as any other candidate. And if he wins he will knock down one more barrier to black people and throughout African American society, children will be able to say, there is nothing I cannot do if I try hard. And that is the vision every civil right leader since the civil war has wanted for blacks in America.

THE PROUD BLACK AMERICAN SOLDIER

The legacy of military valor and achievement by African Americans is truly a source of pride for African Americans in all walks of life. But the changes the military has undergone to accept the presence of black men in uniform has very much mirrored the struggles for integration in society at large.

The history of truly heroic achievements by African American soldiers is just as honorable as any in military history. They include:

March 3, 1770 – The first American to die in the Revolutionary war was a black soldier by the name of Crispus Attucks. He was killed when British soldiers fired on a peaceful gathering in Boston, Massachusetts starting the war that lead to America's independence.

In World War II – Vernon J. Baker took leadership in attacking dug in German machine gun emplacements destroying six and killing twenty six German soldiers. He received the Congressional Medal of Honor for his bravery.

December 7, 1941 – During the horrendous Pearl Harbor attacks, a black galley cook by the name of Dorie Miller on board the USS West Virginia rushed to the deck as his fellow soldiers lay wounded and dying all around him. He valiantly took control of the machine gun emplacement on the deck and repelled the dive bombers keeping them from further killing and injuring his comrades in arms.

For his courage, Dorie Miller received the first Silver Star of World War II.

These are just a few of the hundreds of stories of courage and outstanding service to country made by black men throughout America's history. Within the military, racial prejudice has long gone by the wayside because when men stand side by side in battle, they are brothers first, fellow soldiers second and people of race a distant third if at all. Battle has a way of equalizing all men and real soldiers know that. So the military has been an opportunity to cultivate equality and acceptance because it is a culture where being a good solider is always more important than any petty prejudices any man might carry.

But it took longer for the military as an institution to catch up with what soldiers new instinctively on the battlefield – that all men are equal when they are brothers in arms. Finally on July 26, 1948, President Truman issued Executive Order Number 9981 which stated in no uncertain terms what the U.S. Military's policy was concerning racial segregations...

It is hereby declared to be the policy of the President that there shall be equality of treatment and opportunity for all persons in the armed services without regard to race, color, religion or national origin. This policy shall be put into effect as rapidly as possible, having due regard to the time required to effectuate any necessary changes without impairing efficiency or morale.

We can be grateful for courageous leadership such as President Truman's and for the leadership of the military establishment to set the tone for the eventual social condemnation of segregation. While it is regrettable that American has had to sustain an army to battle her enemies over the centuries, there is no question that the high ethical and moral conduct that is needed for military men to perform in combat follows those men into society when their service to their country is through.

And that is one of the many reasons that the desegregation of the military dictated that not only would racism no longer be tolerated by the American military, it would soon be viewed as ignorant and unacceptable in American society as well. While there is still work to be done to make that dream a reality, accomplishments such as these we have discussed lay the groundwork for a better world of integration for all American citizens.

LAUGHTER THAT HEALS

The great thing about the history of black America and the methods African American leadership has used to seek full equality and acceptance in this country is that there have been many roads to that goal. Yes, the great social, political, legal and even military movements that have been conducted to free African Americans from slavery and achieve full citizenship were crucial. And the great black leadership of dynamic personalities like Martin Luther King and George Washington Carver have made things possible that would never have been possible otherwise.

But not all of the gains in society have been achieved through tears and anger. In fact, some great black leadership can be found in a place one never would think to look. It can be found in the stand-up comedy night clubs and on forward thinking television shows as black comedians helped everybody, black and white, laugh together at the differences in the races rather than cry separately.

Some of the most revered figures in comedy in the last thirty years were from the African American community. There are many notable names that spring immediately to mind that have used the "podium" of a comedy microphone and stage to talk about issues of race, color, discrimination and race relations in a way that all can appreciate their thoughts and achieve a common understanding. The names of Bill Cosby, Richard Pryor, Eddie Murphy and many more stand out as both very funny entertainers and people who have represented the African American community with pride and intelligence that all can admire.

Many African American children took hope from the idea of rising up out of poverty and difficulty to reach greatness because they saw these black entertainers do it. Just by using their success to show the youth of black America that they too can be successful and that with hard work, intelligence, and the willingness to try they too can be somebody to their families and to their community. This is truly the role of a great role model and these men have given much hope to youth to make something of themselves and make a difference.

Sometimes it was hard for these entertainers to achieve equality. When Sammy Davis Junior first was recruited to make his valuable contribution to Frank Sinatra's team, many in that society did not think it was appropriate that a black man could perform with equality with his white contemporaries. We can be grateful too for the openness of others in the entertainment community that they would not stand to see racism keep talent such as Sammy's down. It was Sinatra himself that made sure that Sammy Davis could perform with the "Rat Pack" and in doing so, another door of racism was blown down in this country.

Stories like these are frequent. The Hollywood establishment always has been forward thinking in presenting entertainers based on their talent and not on the color of their skin or other artificial divisions. It has been television as well that has broken barriers and open the discussion of race and color for all of us to engage. By making it "ok" to talk about race relations, it also makes it ok to see those relations healed and clear the way for reconciliation and healing.

Many times, when a black comedian is making his crowd laugh, he might say "the important thing is we talk about these things and laugh about them together". And that is the important thing. We can be grateful we have had such outstanding leadership in entertainment to bring black and white together in a way that eliminates hatred and hostility. Because it is hard to hate your brother when you are busy laughing together with him.

(Refer to my book- Just Stand Up: The History of Black Comedians for more information on this subject.)

THE THIRTEENTH AMENDMENT

Looking back on it now, it's almost amazing to any modern American that we ever needed something like The Thirteenth Amendment. The very fact that the United States government had to take this step to outlaw slavery in this country once and for all tells us that the more liberated way we think in modern times was not always the way life was viewed just a few hundred years ago. In light of the long uphill struggle black history in this country represents, it is worthwhile to look back at this simple but powerful amendment which simply states...

Neither slavery nor involuntary servitude, except as a punishment for crime whereof the party shall have been duly convicted, shall exist within the United States, or any place subject to their jurisdiction.

This amendment to the constitution of the United States, along with the fourteenth and fifteenth amendments represent the most dramatic changes to the fundamental law of this land in regards to civil rights in American history. And it took strong and courageous leadership by Abraham Lincoln to assure that these provisions were so imbedded into the core definition of what America was and is that there would never be a chance that slavery would rise again inside our borders.

The date to remember of the passage of this history Amendment is April 8, 1864. It was the end of the civil war and the south lay in defeat, still separated from the north before reconstruction could begin the long task of making this nation one again. The wisdom President Lincoln had to take action while the sounds of battle were still fresh in the ears of all Americans to set in stone the achievements of this bloody war cannot be overlooked.

Up until the Civil War, slavery was a common part of American life. It is painful for all Americans, black and white, to look back on a time when most Americans considered it normal for one human being to own another. While the many great strides for civil rights and equality in the decades to come would stand tall in black history, this very basic restoration of the right of African Americans to be treated as humans had to be a fundamental start to becoming full citizens of this great land.

And so with the guns of the Civil War just recently silenced by the North's victory, President Lincoln moved swiftly to make slavery a thing of the past forever. First, in 1863, he issued "The Emancipation Proclamation" stating in no uncertain terms that...

> *"all persons held as slaves within any State, or designated part of a State, the people whereof shall then be in rebellion against the United States, shall be then, thenceforward, and forever free."*

But despite the power of this proclamation, Lincoln knew that The Constitution had to be amended to make the good intent of the Emancipation Proclamation the irrevocable law of the land. And so he championed The Thirteen Amendment through congress to assure that it was made law and that slavery could never again become a common and accepted part of American life.

It was an important start. But we all know that true freedom was still had many more battles ahead of it. When slave owners around the country, released their slaves, African Americans everywhere knew a freedom they had only dreamed of before. But it was just one step in a long uphill struggle for equality and freedom that continues on to this day.

Let us all look back on President Lincoln's vision, forward thinking and courage and let it inspire similar vision and courage in us to find ways to make American society free and equal for all citizens, black, white and for all races, creeds and colors. If we can achieve that, then we have done our part to join President Lincoln in seeking freedom for all men.

THE FIFTEENTH AMENDMENT

When the Civil War came to an end, it was important to take the big accomplishments and transition them into the law of the land before any ground was lost as reconstruction returned the nation to one country rather than two warring parties. The upheaval of society that the abolition of slavery represented and the massive surge forward for black history was so important that it was important to make it permanent with amendments to the constitution so the gains made during that bloody battle would not be lost again.

The work that needed to be done to change a nation from one of slavery to one of equality started with three important amendments to the constitution. The thirteenth amendment abolished slavery forever and the fourteenth amendment reversed the negative effects of the Dred Scott decision providing equal protection under the law for all citizens of this country regardless of race, color or creed.

But the Fifteenth Amendment went further than just establishing the basic human rights of the African American community. It made a change so fundamental to how America works that its ramifications were sweeping and far reaching down to this day. The text of the amendment is direct and elegant...

> *The right of citizens of the United States to vote shall not be denied or abridged by the United States or by any State on account of race, color, or previous condition of servitude.*

This was a tremendous leap forward for the black community when this amendment was ratified on February 3, 1870 because it finally meant that the African American population in this country could stand up and be counted and start making a mark on politics and with it how decisions are made in this country. It was a proud moment when the very first black man to cast a vote came the very next day when Thomas Mundy Peterson voted in a school board election in the town of Perth Amboy, New Jersey

But like so many other great advances in black history, earning the right to vote didn't automatically make it easy to vote. There was staunch resistance to actually allowing blacks to go to the polling booth in many communities across the country. The Klu Klux Klan engaged in intimidation tactics to try to keep African Americans home from the polls. In Louisiana, the mob attempts to stop the institutions of a legally elected and integrated local governments had to be broken up by federal troops sent in by Ulysses S. Grant.

Probably the most serious threat to the actual workability of the fifteenth amendment was the introduction of the poll tax and other registration tricks that were used such as literacy tests and voter qualification tests clearly designed to deny the right to vote to African Americans. This practice became such a problem that it instigated the passage of the twenty fourth amendment which outlawed poll taxes which were only designed to usurp the rights of African Americans to vote.

But these desperate attempts could not stop the march of justice and democracy to assure that voting rights were available to all Americans. Before long blacks were occupying positions of influence and decision making in state legislatures and even at the federal level. It's been a long struggle but even in the last few decades we have seen positions of high honor and influence held by qualified African Americans such as Barack Obama, Colin Powell and Condoleezza Rice.

THE RAINBOW COALITION

The struggle for freedom and equality for African Americans is one that is passed down from generation to generation and from one era of black leadership to the next. Throughout history, the African American leadership has had many outstanding men and women who made their mark and made a difference for black people in America. And that tradition continues to this day with modern black leadership such as Barrack Obama, The Reverend Al Sharpton and Jessie Jackson.

Jessie Jackson has organized his efforts to continue the struggle for civil rights in one of the most innovative organizations in history that came to be known as the Rainbow Coalition. This organization represented the dreams and goals of the Reverend Jackson, to be sure. But it also represents the shared efforts of black Americans across the country in modern times to keep the dream of Martin Luther King alive and moving forward.

In fact, the Rainbow Coalition was the outcome of a series of efforts and movements that began with a relationship between Reverend Jackson and Dr. King. It was Martin Luther King that asked Jessie Jackson to head up a movement called Operation Breadbasket, a project to seek the economic improvement of black communities across the country, particularly in the inner city. Operation Bread- basket eventually evolved into a powerful civil rights organization known as the Southern Christian Leadership Conference.

As these movements started to make a real difference in the lives of African Americans in America, another step was the development of Operation PUSH which stood for People United to Save Humanity. This influential organization has become the cornerstone for promoting civil rights and social justice for African Americans in the last twenty years.

It was from these different initiatives and the success they were realizing that the Rainbow Coalition was birthed to seek economic opportunity in the business community and to encourage Fortune 500 companies to hire minorities and to expand their involvement in the nurture and the development of black community for the good of all peoples.

The naming of the movement "The Rainbow Coalition" is pivotal to the vision Reverend Jackson had for the civil rights movement. He did not see it as just black people working for the betterment of the black community. Instead, inspired by Martin Luther King's dream of equality and brotherhood of all races, the coalition would truly be a partnership of all minorities, the white community and other equal rights movements to seek equal opportunity for all of America's citizens.

The important stance that The Rainbow Coalition brought to the consciousness of the black community and to America was the concept that civil rights was not just a black issue. It emphasized that all of America cannot move foreword when a part of the population is left behind to flounder in poverty and without the benefits of a good education and job opportunities. The result is that the black pride that was built by key figures of black history such as Mohammed Ali, Spike Lee and even more radical elements such as Malcolm X and the Black Panthers could now be used to promote true equality in the society. In doing so, Jackson and other contemporary black leaders taught that the African American community not only could be but must insist on being fully black and fully American in their status in American culture.

Finally, the Rainbow Coalition emphasized that civil rights is not just a political issue. The emphasis was on all aspects of American life including economic equality, social opportunity and even equal representation in the media and entertainment arts. To be truly represented as an important part of American culture, black Americans must have equal opportunities in all venues.

This is the message for its time that Reverend Jackson and the Rainbow coalition has brought and continues to bring to the national stage. And it's an important message that takes the good that was done in past civil rights movements in this country and brings up to date with a new century.

AFTERWORD

Throughout black history, great black athletes have served as role models to America's youth, in a way that may not have been possible for others leaders. And to be sure, some of these great heroes of athletics have become virtually godlike to all sports fans, not just those in the black community. Michael Jordan's ability on the basketball field during his career at times seems to be virtually super-human. And the career of Mohammed Ali sent such a powerful message of black pride to black and white America that he virtually transformed social perception of the black man through sheer talent and attitude.

Before Muhammad Ali came along, the idea of a black boxer, even a very good black boxer becoming such a central figure for black pride seemed unlikely. But Ali demonstrated something to the youth of the African American community that was so inspirational that it helped to transform their world view like no other public figure could have done.

With his swagger and braggadocio, Ali stood out as a proud black man in such a way that had never been seen before. His use of rhyme with such phrases as "I float like a butterfly and sting like a bee" to his self promotion maintaining "I'm pretty", that sent a message to black and white admirer alike. And that message was loud and clear. Ali was black and he was proud and other black men and women in America have just as much reason to be proud as he was.

This was an important message because coming out of years of oppression, it was sometimes difficult for black youth to gain a sense of pride and the self assurance needed to get out there and be a success. It took the work of great black role models such as Mohammed Ali to let them know that it is allowable for you to be proud and to be great as well. For Ali didn't back up his claims with just boasts. He was truly a great black athlete as well. So when Ali bragged that he was "pretty" showing that the way he fought truly was a thing of beauty.

That same excellence and how it has been used to inspire the black community can be found in the phenomenal career of Michael Jordan. In the same way that Ali's talent seemed to eclipse even the genre of boxing, Jordan was so phenomenal at basketball that he became an icon of excellence and skill and a role model for black youth across the country. Both of these men recognized that God had given them this tremendous talent and the opportunities to reach their potential. And they worked hard to be a role model to their community so others would be inspired to be their best as well.

Moreover, great black sports heroes also provided healing by setting a high standard of excellence for sports fans of all races to admire. It wasn't just black sports fans who adored the work of Mohammed Ali and Michael Jordan. They became true heroes to anyone to whom sports was an important part of life.

The field of sports is an arena where men and woman can come to socialize and find common ground. Like entertainment, there is a world of sports that makes comrades of all who enjoy the exploits of sports heroes whether on the baseball diamond, the football field, the boxing arena or the basketball stadium. And sports fans have a standard that they value their heroes that is based on talent, achievement and ability to do that one thing everybody in sports admires–to be a winner. And Mohammed Ali and Michael Jordan were certainly embodiment of great black men who were also in every way winners. And we all admire that regardless of race, color or creed.

www.ingramcontent.com/pod-product-compliance
Lightning Source LLC
Chambersburg PA
CBHW071021080526
44587CB00015B/2442